The Betrayed Town
&
Other Poems

Roselyne M. Jua

Langaa Research & Publishing CIG
Mankon, Bamenda

Publisher
Langaa RPCIG
Langaa Research & Publishing Common Initiative Group
P.O. Box 902 Mankon
Bamenda
North West Region
Cameroon
Langaagrp@gmail.com
www.langaa-rpcig.net

Distributed in and outside N. America by African Books Collective
orders@africanbookscollective.com
www.africanbookcollective.com

ISBN: 9956-728-61-6

About the Poet

Roselyne M. Jua holds a BA (Hons) from Carleton University, Ottawa, Canada and a PhD from the State University of New York at Buffalo, New York, otherwise known by the acronym SUNY, Buffalo. She has taught English and American Literature and Creative Writing at the Universities of Yaounde (1986-1993) and Buea (1993-2012). In Buea she held various administrative posts: Head of the Department of English; Head of Division for Teaching and Teaching Staff; Vice-Dean in charge of Studies and Students' Affairs; and more recently from 2010 to 2012 Vice-Dean of Programmes and Academic Affairs, a post she held cumulatively with that of Acting–Dean, Faculty of Arts. She was appointed Director of Academic affairs in August 2012 at the newly created University of Bamenda, North West Region.

A 2001 Senior Fulbright Research Fellow her research interest focuses on literature and space with the underpinnings for identity, recognition and authenticity. She has reviewed several books, published articles in peer-reviewed journals and edited the plays of Victor E. Musinga among which are *The Barn* and *The Tragedy of Mr. No-Balance*. She is co-author with Bate Besong of *To the Budding Creative Writer: A Handbook*. Interested in development issues she is presently coordinator for a CODESRIA sponsored multidisciplinary project on four women's groups in the North West Region of Cameroon. She has as team member for AAI observed Legislative and Presidential Elections in several African countries: Madagascar, Uganda, Guinea – Conakry and Ivory Coast.

Dedication

To Alan Tamu-Jua Ngwa, Erico Che-Ngom Ngwa and Erika Bih-Lai Ngwa in the belief that your house is built on solid rock.

Table of Contents

Acknowledgment

I want to thank my daughter Erika for permission, once again, to make use of one of her paintings for the cover to this book. I say once again because I had done so in the handbook entitled *To the Budding Creative Writer,* (with her permission) but failed to acknowledge her work there.

One of her untitled works also graces the cover of George D. Nyamndi's *Dogs in the Sun.*

Preface

I began writing poetry some thirty-five years ago and so by 1990 I had quite a sizeable collection. But I remained for the most part a closet writer, even though I would in 1977 send out one of my first poems entitled "The Betrayed Town" and it would be accepted for publication in *The Anthology of Unpublished Poets*, Riverview, Florida. This and my father's ecstatic response to my endeavors encouraged me to continue. Interestingly enough, visitors to my room in Renfrew House at Carleton University, Ottawa, would themselves be exposed to some of these poems, which begged to be read as they smiled down from the walls.

In my undergraduate years at Carleton, Dr. Siga Asanga would read some of the poems and write a critique. I recall that he was particularly impressed with the vignettes. Professor Victor Anomah Ngu would visit Ottawa, read some of the poems and encourage me to keep writing. Even after I returned home finally after my doctoral studies in 1984, every time we met, one of the first things he was sure to ask me was whether I had finally published my poems. Presenting him with a published copy of the book would have been my way of saying "thank you" to him for the encouragement. Sad to say this would not be possible since he died in 2011.

I did not know when or if I ever would gather courage and the nerve to send the collection out for publication! In 1981, when I took a postgraduate course in Creative Writing I was finally forced to share some of my work with Professor Irving Feldman and my classmates at SUNY, Buffalo.

Professor Leslie A. Fiedler, supervisor of my PhD dissertation at SUNY also read some of the poems and advised me to send them out to publishers. My famous response was that I would think about it. Even after I graduated from Buffalo, when I called him up on the phone one of the questions he was sure to ask me was whether I had finally made up to mind to do so. When I finally did make up my mind to do so, I could no longer carry on a long conversation with him for he was already seriously sick. I will be forever grateful to him for his continuing effort to encourage me to bring my work out.

A culmination of events has brought me to this pass. Most of my poems having been composed in long hand, because I could only hunt and peck at the typewriter, the tedium of doing so which at the time could only be borne when a term paper was concerned, for as the proverbial student money was usually in short supply, I usually traveled with sheaves of writing, proofing and editing whenever or wherever I could. But election monitoring is a funny thing and in the mad rush to get out of Guinea-Conakry, where our team report was in complete dissonance with published government opinion, I would forget the bulk of my sweat back at the hotel. I can only hope that this forgotten sheaf of poems will have brought a smile to someone's lips. But I am more than certain that they probably found their way only to the trash since they were written in English. What a waste! Learning to use the computer became a priority if I was to ascertain that I would not lose those that I could find or recall. The more poems I entered the more the idea of a book took hold as I exclaimed like the old man of "Panda Games," "What the heck!" But not to hoist a beer! I would hoist a soda.

Ralph Ellison or rather what happened to his manuscript for *Juneteenth* was a great signifier to me if I did not want to lose everything. It was time indeed for me to come in from the cold!

In 2002, when I returned from my Senior Fulbright year at Howard University, Washington D.C., I had come to a decisive moment and sent the poems to John A. Lambo, Professor of English Literature at the University of Yaoundé I for his critical opinion. A busy man, teaching full time at the university and working full time at the Ministry of Higher Education, he none-the-less read through the poems and called me up to say that I had better publish them. I said to him, "You had better write the foreword to the collection if it would not be a further imposition on your time." His response was that he would gladly do so but that it may take a while. It was to take a while. I would see him during the University Games in Yaoundé in May 2003 and he would promise sending that foreword to me as soon as the games were over. He would himself bring the foreword to Buea where he was attending a meeting in June, one month later. A week later, we would meet in Yaoundé where we were both attending a meeting and he would confess that he had had to search for the poems in his office for quite a while because he felt too embarrassed to call and ask me for another copy of the work. He confessed when we discussed his foreword to the poems that he had toned down certain sections of his appreciation because as he claimed they reflected too much his joy at reading the poems, and he did not want that to be misconstrued. Then, he would not have done justice to my work, he opined. He would die three days later. It is only right that I mention here that a few of the poems in this collection were written after John died. Calling him by his first name is a liberty I enjoyed while he was alive and I have seen no reason why I should give it up at this time.

Returning to Cameroon upon completion of my doctoral studies in 1984, I would be recruited after a lot of wrangling, focusing on my provenance of origin and my so called youth, to teach English and American Literature at the University of Yaoundé where John was already a senior colleague teaching English poetry. I want to acknowledge John's encouragement here for telling me in no uncertain terms that what I write can bring pleasure to anyone who listens closely. I had willy-nilly come face to face with problems of ethnicity and sexism in my own country, problems I had associated only with distant shores. If I had grown up in a cocoon in Buea making no distinctions between my friends with no care as to their origins, the scales simply dissolved from my eyes. This was my reality check, my welcome home and what a welcome it was.

The title of this book, like for many of the poems therein, has gone through various permutations, the most prominent among which was *In My Father's House*. I thought this title befitting not only for the sound but also for the possibilities it opened up. Helas, it was not to be.

This, in brief, is the story behind my work. In bringing it to public notice I make an offering of the diverse rooms of my experiences.

RMJ
Bamenda
10 September 2012

Foreword

I really enjoyed perusing Roselyne Jua's collection of what, for want of a more illuminating expression, may be described as a rich variety of poems in which she sings to the tune of the music of her own soul on subjects as diverse as nature, nostalgia, prostitution, the sense of loss, exploitation, nonchalance, and so forth.

She writes poetry into which she movingly pours her grief and frustrations, resulting from certain practices and occurrences, such as the sempiternal "File chasing" or "hunting phenomenon" and the shabby treatment the "hunter" receives; the inability of Anglophones to speak French well and so are snubbed, ridiculed by their so-called Francophone brothers; the animosity that indigenes of certain areas nurse towards those who have come to be known as "settlers," an "inimical" term used to describe fellow countrymen whose only crime, ironically, is their hard work, resourcefulness and the development of hitherto neglected areas and lands.

In "Midnight Girl," Jua takes on prostitution, exhorting drifters to be aware of girls who hang around the streets at night, for the prostitutes' gorgeous and fashionable outward appearance invariably veneers "crevices of …sagging and layered body." One notices here that in one dazzling expression the poetess summarily delineates a putrefied society where men and women, caught, as it were, in a labyrinth of vices and immorality, have lost every sense of decency.

Values, she holds, have indeed been turned inside out. Culturally, the sharing of kola-nuts was, as in the days of yore, a sign of friendship and, to borrow from Chinua Achebe, a symbol of living peace among true friends, but today in Africa people disguise their betrayal of so-called friends by sharing kola-nuts with them. Turn your back and these "friends" are in bed with your wife and your husband. The experience described in "the kola-nut" recalls Shakespeare's warning: "There's daggers in men's smiles."

Jua's grief and frustrations overflow to poems that focus overtly on politico-economic issues. Democracy, she claims, does not seem to find a fertile ground in Africa, as long as "Half-baked politicians and partisan journalists" continue to victimise and oppress "those of differing leanings," democracy can never grow and mature enough to yield the required fruits, to wit, development, national wealth and the well being of the greatest number.

The poetess' sense of regret for "coming back home" is couched in very subtle and highly metaphorical terms in "Mother Nyos" where the lake is personified as a deceptive mother who lures her children back home only to kill them. This intricate state of things is tellingly captured in the expressions "lush enticing greenery," "Summoning to a mortal embrace." Like a leadless pencil, the home-comers, as suggested in "My Pencil, Myself," have lost themselves and so feel worthless and damned, deprived, so to say, of their erstwhile sweet and peaceful "Sleep of the lotus eaters." Is the issue involved here "Unification?"

Jua frowns upon this historical event, even as she remonstrates, as clearly expressed in "Ode to Farmers," against the non-remuneration of farmers who toil all day and all year long for "Nothing." The farmers and their families live in abject poverty and squalor, while their exploiters, those who feed fat on their labour, seen in terms of their castles, of what they eat, drink and wear, live a life that is thoroughly extravagant. Unable to suppress her emotions in the face of such injustice, the poetess, in the manner of Percy Bysshe Shelley, cries out in a tone that is unmistakably revolutionary: "You must be paid …Now!" in a world where all too many forces are unfriendly and repressive, Jua speaks still for love, justice and freedom. One is tempted here to consider mother hen, whose young, she has lost to the eagle as representing the oppressed who are ready to stand up for their rights.

Nostalgia, the recollection of happy moments of the halcyon past, is the subject of some of Jua's poems, one of which is "The Lodge," referring, I suppose, to the Prime Minister's Lodge in Buea where the poetess spent her childhood. Written in Ottawa in 1978, the poem expresses the poetess' anxiety about the present state of this historical edifice of seventy-two rooms that stands alone by the mountainside, probably uninhabited, with the furniture worn out, the garden uncared for and no children playing around.

The same nostalgic sentiments are voiced in "A Lament" in which she fondly recalls the happy countryside of Buea, her "eternal home." The main feature of the countryside which impresses itself on her imagination is the Chariot of the gods, towering over hills and valleys," inspiring "harmony and peace." However, underneath this apparently happy state of things, Jua feels a certain sense of emptiness, a certain void, as suggested by the oxymoronic "roaring silence" around. One is tempted here to associate Jua with the Keatsian "negative capability," the propensity of viewing existence as a complex network of paradoxes, a union of opposites, a marriage of "Heaven and Hell," to borrow William Blake's consecrated expression of this phenomenon.

In spite of the sense of void mentioned heretofore, the poetess prefers the past to the sordid present. "Up the Hill," a poem in which she expresses the desire to turn back the clock, clearly shows a certain exhilarating preference for the "peace and quiet" of the past when she drank of the fresh waters of the lake, enjoyed watching the "evergreen trees" and listening to the "twittering birds," the "rustling of winds" and the message of the drums.

Jua has a good eye for the natural world and still a better one for details, for particular places, situations and events. This is true of the poems discussed thus far, even as it is with the bulk of her poems. There is, for instance, "The River" whose overflowing banks, "rippling, sighing and lappings" make her heart vibrate. The Menchum Falls mesmerizes everything around, including the poetess, inspiring in them a sense of awe. Her robust admiration of the natural phenomenon is however mitigated by the thought that the fall, powerful enough to light the whole of Africa, is yet to be valorised, exploited in this regard. The expression, "Sinking, falling, never to arise/ in the depths of dark forgotten Africa" captures in vividly plaintive and cynical terms Jua's heartfelt concerns with man's negligence and visionlessness.

The Rain Maker's cry that causes rain to fall in abundance, engendering the bushes to grow thick and so give rise to a situation that pits the young against the old; the fact that women love travelling with "excess baggage; the "snake soldiers in trenches/stinking trenches" bent on paying back vice for vice, a proclivity that defies the more ennobling virtue of forgiveness; the Whitesands of Mombassa and the "white foams" of the Indies as well as the vendors who cheat tourists by tripling the prices of "Kangas and Kitenges," are all details of places, events and situations for which the poetess has a keen eye. "Farewell" is another poem which recalls memories of the past, but this time Jua is concerned with a rather personal predicament – the loss of her father, a loss that is rendered even more regretful and terrible by the fact that she could not attend the burial ceremony, being thousands of miles away in the Canada. Albeit, she is now left only with a mind evaded by flitting images of the past, a perturbed heart that could not say that important last farewell to the father, his spirit however, communes with her, curbing and sobering, as it were, her restiveness. Jua seems to be insinuating here that, though dead, the father still watches over his loved ones, guarding them and ensuring their general success in life. This belief in ancestral guardianship, as with the transmigration of souls, is central to African traditional religion.

In spite of the strong indignation Jua feels against injustice, misconduct and the absence of foresightedness in society, she is capable of rising up, as indicated in "Le Bosquet," in praise of hilarious Africa, throbbing with life, vibrating with music and dance and replete with spectacle and nourishment. Jua laughs at others, but she is not incapable of laughing at herself - confer "Excess Luggage," "Vigilance" and "The Ritual." It is true, poems of this nature do not bulk large in her collection, but their very presence in it suggests, happily, a balanced and honest attitude towards life, life as an interminable process of becoming. The vexing issues she writes on do not reduce her to pessimistic indifference and despondency far from it!

Suffice it to say, in conclusion, that the statements I have made about Roselyne Jua's poems are far from being exhaustive and less so definitive. If the deconstructionist theory of literature is anything to go by, no single statement or meaning can be assigned to a literary text, in view of the very dynamic nature of life, marked by ironies, ambiguities and paradoxes. I therefore invite students, teachers and the general readership to read and reread this beautiful collection of poems, bringing their personal intellectual experiences to bear on them.

John Akwe LAMBO
Professor of English Literature
University of Yaoundé I
Cameroon

An Appreciation

In a world where the lurid and dramatic have become the standard fare in representations of Africa, it is refreshing to read poems such as Roselyn Jua's which depict the continent as a land of ordinary people, living ordinary lives, partaking in the ordinary nostalgias and anxieties, the everyday joys and sorrows that beset ordinary people everywhere in the world. Perhaps, the truly remarkable, distinguishing feature of the poems collected in this volume is this focus on the ordinary, everyday experience, devoid of the dramatic violence and genocidal conflict that have become the norm in narratives about Africa. Indeed, in these poems, the speaking voice guides us through a poetic experience that enjoins us to look out for the 'insignificant' detail that produces profound insight, to listen for the nuance of language where meaning arises out of paradox, irony, and understatement rather than through the hyperbolic, overladen word. It is only by cultivating a stance of complex looking and listening in this manner that we will come to a deeper appreciation of the fuller import of these poems.

I do not wish to repeat the themes of Professor John Akwe Lambo's excellent foreword to the collection. However, in this brief appreciation, I wish to draw attention to one important point that will enrich the experience of reading these poems. This, I believe, relates to the art of poetry itself. If one of the strengths of poetry as a genre is its ability to let us into a world of profound, symbolic meaning through the invocation of the concrete image, these poems provide us memorable examples of this. In a poem such as "My Poor Pencil, My Poor Self," we apprehend, in the image of the pencil that has been hollowed out of its lead, a host of symbolic themes, such as the relationship between writing and the modern self, between wholeness and alienation, the splitting of the self and the falling into pieces of the subject, and a wide array of psycho-analytical conditions suffered by those denied voice, speech, subjectivity, etc. Now, imagine, what a pedagogic journey of close reading and interpretation we could undertake analyzing this brief 10-line imagistic poem. This is but one example of the kinds of symbolic ripples that a concise and lucid poem such as this - focused on mining a single image – can produce.

I want to go further to suggest that what remains with us – at least, certainly with me – after reading Roselyne Jua's poems is the haunting presence in each poem of a single image, a single event or situation, through which a wealth of symbolic meanings emerge. Whether it is the Czech girl in "Meanings" learning and living in a foreign language through gesture and sound or the hardworking women and lazying husbands in "A Perfect Setting" or "Lawino's Daughter's Song" or the reminiscences of another time and place encapsulated in poems such as "The Lodge" and "Up the Hill," it is this centrality of the image to the poetic exploration that endures. This is a poetic technique that eschews the grand statement and the unanchored abstraction but rather underscores the juxtaposition of the concrete and the symbolic and abstract as its dominant representational strategy.

Having been a "closet poet" for so long – to use the poet's own words – it is surely time that Roselyne Jua's poems entered into the public domain and be welcome by a larger, appreciative audience.

Harry Garuba
University of Cape Town, 2012

In my Father's house are many mansions

John 14: 2

Going to farm

If running across two sticks embracing the earth were that easy
I would do it.
My aunt must look back and call out to me to join her
Wondering why this sister's child has turned her back—
Now, she must make the trip back to bring her over—

Place your right foot and left foot parallel to your body
To grip the logs; try once more. Yes, yes, that's it.
Now, don't look down as you traverse the logs.
Look straight across to the other side,
Keep your feet focused on the logs and your grip.

How do you cross over a gorge?
Between you and the silvery meandering stream
No love lost, only one hundred feet of bottomless nothing
How do you grip ball-like logs with sandals?
Take off the sandals of course!
How do you not look down into the mesmerizing clean waters!
One false move and –
This my second lesson for the morning.
Imaginings had elicited the first trudging down one hill
Sliding down a second and third—
How was I going to get up these same mountains?
How carry a full basket of corn?
How carry a full basket of corn across my mimesis?
How carry a full basket of corn across with footwork to remember?
Carry/corn
Cross/stream carrying a basket of corn

Climb up four hills carrying a basket of corn!
So so many lessons to learn in one day
Rivers to cross
Logs to hug
Hills, No! Mountains to crawl up!

No, I will not carry a basket of corn!
Your hand must guide me once more across the stream,
Across the ball-like eucalyptus which feet must hug.
Let me creep up the hills, sliding, panting, asking,
Who sent you?
But, I will not carry any corn
Laughing stork or not of my youngest cousin.
So many occasions sliding and sitting
My once beige dress dyed beyond recognition
My feet cakes of mud
Brown logs fit for the fire
Fire to roast brown fresh corn
Rub melted butter and salivate
Then eat to your fill and go to sleep
If the bugs would let you.

                                        Njinikom, 1974

Justice

I am thinking about my "pays."
If I were to go from town to town
Will I have covered the land?
And, from Ministry to Ministry,
Minister to Minister,
Office to Office
Officers to Officers
File through File,
Will I say I have s'n "l'etat"--

But, if I were to go
From President to Vice
Minister to Vice
Right to the office hag
Who will not tell me
Who will not shout at me
Maybe even shoot at me
 Of course, you have s'n the land!

But what is the land --
Is it the towns
Or the Ministers and their ministries,
the Officers
then their files
and their vices!
Have I s'n the people
And is the land not just the people!
But where are the people?

U of Manitoba, Winnipeg, 1975

Excess Baggage

One suitcase had my brother
I, two.
Journeying but for a week
I filled the boot
A third saw the light of day
 For the rest, darkness.
Tell me, Why women do
With excess baggage travel
When less would suffice?

Winnipeg, 1975

Meanings

Dasha from Czechoslovakia had come to Winnipeg to study
English
One fine day in class her name became "Beckon"
For she laughed and asked, what is that?
What does it mean?
And I raised my hands and flipped my forefinger twice at her
And I asked, What does that mean?
And she said, Oh, is that what that means?
And as Al Purdy read from his poems
She ohed! and ahed! All through class,
And I asked why the moaning? And she retorted,
What do you mean? And I ohed! And ahed! just like her,
And she said, Oh! Is that what that means?
But I did not answer her for I was busy reading the clipboard,
Then she nudged me, and I screamed, Dasha that was not a
nudge!
That hurt!!
And she asked, what is that? What does that mean?
So, I gave it back to her, and she wailed
Ohhhh! Is that what that means!
Bearing our folders we trudged through white mountains
To freshman composition to learn more new words,
Wondering if we would ever write like Al Purdy!!!

Winnipeg, 1975

5

Camouflage

Green spots
grey spots
brown spots
black spots

Soldiers on their bellies
on the ground
The man, the snake
Soldiers in the trenches
stinking trenches
Soldiers planted behind --
Vice against vice
Firing in unison
The hiss of the smelting void
The triumph of the ultimate
But a H-I-S-S
Gasped in the very entrails of dust!

Winnipeg, 1975

Vigilance

As I castigate myself
The heavy dough out stares me,
Watching quietly as I rant and curse
Defeated, I acknowledge my neglect,
Wonder at my own stupidity,
Double over with laughter,
Toss the evidence in the trash
And profess future vigilance.

                                        Winnipeg, 1975

Lost and Found

Can't even find my way to the ticket office--
Where's the ticket office Mister?
Quoi -- Qu'est ce que tu dis ?
Can you tell me where the ticket office is?
Je ne te comprends pas, Monsieur.
GONE
Lost.
No hope of redemption
Betrayed into bandying phrases
Recollected from ages past.
Was it 10
            15
                20
or thirty years ago?
The word for ticket is billet-something
Or is it fish (he's thinking of fiche)
"Billet," that's it.

"Acheter," is not difficult.
Everyone does that.
The President does that.
The ministers do that.
The office hag does that.
Everyone indeed does that.
They are people too!
One is either doing this or 'vendre'
                    (he forgets the 'se' preceding)
But who cares!
Would my old acquaintance think me senile?
Would it scare him if I were to walk up softly?

- -Pouvez-vous m'aider, mon fils? —

Ottawa, 1976

I saw a woodpecker today

I saw a woodpecker today
Edging its way up a tree.
I looked the other way,
An eagle hovered nearby.
I heard mother hen calling its young
Knew the hunter had picked its prey.
Then he swooped !

Looking up,
I saw the helpless infant borne swiftly away.
But, I did not catch one sound
And knew it had defied its mother
-- an easy prey on its own --
Only mother hen furiously clucking
She had lost one of her young.
Feathers and wings stuck out,
She was ready for the big war.

Carleton University, Ottawa, 1976

My poor pencil, My poor self

You were whole until
I bore a hole through you
My poor pencil
My poor self
I took the lead away
Split it into pieces
And threw them all away-
Now, I have the shell of a pencil
And therefore cannot write.
Where then, is myself?

Ottawa, November 8, 1976

Changing

My cushioned chair stands by my desk
It is made of wood
And has four legs.
If I were to curl my legs
I could put them through a bridge
High above the floor.
But , I would have to sit front to back
I refuse to try as I read
And anyway, what's the use of changing!

December 5, 1976

The Betrayed Town

Like bees boozing over honey making
So does the seashore hum with life
With the town quiet in the background
But for the early morning call
Of the one barefooted little girl
Carrying a tray on her head
Summoning you from the regions of Orpheus –
Fine, fine akara di go!
Fine, fine agidi di go!
You turn over and mutter in sleep
To show your clock you can beat it
Settle down for another doze and snore
And dream of the little town
With its big shops, magical names and wide streets
Where people were always so friendly --
You smile in your sleep

11

Start running to the harbor
And the new ship, the new ship always in the offing
Disappears with the buzz of bitter alarm!

Ottawa, 1976, 1980

The Tunnel

Walking through the tunnels
On our way to supper
I danced and hopped.
You started to comment --
Only what you did was read

    Cock-sucker
--The writing on the wall --
First shock. Then quiet.
It had this soothing effect -
The two words flow and infuse
And you must listen hard for that tautness
The tension it produces and embraces
And then be startled off your feet
The next moment by an explosion!

Carleton University, 1976

Taboo

First, one
Then another
I suck the sweets
I spied
In the dark dark deep recesses
of the lady's hidden painted jar
remarking that they were almost stale.

Ottawa, 1977

A Lament

For having been watched over
              and listened to by you,
For nursing me when I was sick
No matter the tantrums,
For all these things and much more
I will always be thankful
My true friend.
My eternal home.
My very own mountain in Buea
Encompassing the hills and valleys
-- One huge happy countryside --

Lulled, believing an infinity of harmony and peace
We pandered to our every wish
Then marveled at the emptiness
Drowning in our drunken stupor amidst
The roaring silence of the countryside.
Yes, I was rendered a fool in my innocence

13

By the deep muffled hush of the countryside.

Ottawa, 1977

Damned

Fallen,
>   Exiled,
>   Degraded --
Fallen from the sin of Adam
Fallen from the greed of Eve
The sin of MAN
Creation and destruction
Disinterested Benevolence
Gulled by the hissing serpent
Exiled from sleep
The sleep of the lotus-eaters
Shocked,
Forced to an awakening,
Then, damned!
If I have lost my innocence,
So have you and you and you.
For how build only to destroy?
The serpent's tongue beguiling you,
Reducing to a bundle of paranoia!
Enemies made of former consorts,
Self-deceiving bloated self-righteousness,
You are either with me or against me!
I am always right—
I know it all—
My views must be your views,
One a puppet to the other
Ensuring loss of identity—

How can you live among men and hold such views?
Such intransigence we meet with and fight
Where is your humility?

Panda Games

"Get your ass out of my beer," Purdy says
"Don't retch on my lawn," the man says
Knows it won't make no difference
It has been ten long years
He even shouts at his dog
--Don't you shit on my yard--
If the students don't heed him
Why should the dog?
It is not housebroken

It's the ritual of Panda Games.
The man comes out to watch.
Every year he mumbles
" I ought to move away from here."
But what's one day in a year?
Resigned, he lets the kids have their fun
Says, "What the heck," and hoists a beer.

Ottawa, September 24, 1978

Up the hill

Why should I gazing from my height
Dream of things, which no longer are?
Yesterday OH! So, so long ago
I could drink in your unadulterated freshness
The crystal clear waters of your lake
Quenched my thirst, cooled my aching head.
Your spreading evergreen trees,
Full of the laughter of youth
The twittering of birds
The cool rustling of the winds
And the message of the drums
Ample Shelter --
Will I ever forget that moment
When the car grunting up the hill
Seized and ceased my peace and quiet?
A victim of my own growth!
Can I turn back the clock
And so re-live my perfection!
Am I cursed
 To dream forever of my hut halfway up the hill?
Bewitched into a trance
Hallucinating even when awake!!

Ottawa, 1978

The Lodge

"The Lodge," they call it
With its seventy-two rooms!
The beggar cannot get through
He does not know the password
And never will.
Built during the rule of Puttkammer
It is now the Prime Minister's residence
Or is it ?
It now stands empty.
The silver and furniture polished daily --
I wonder how the flowers fare
If their odors still pervade the rooms
And where is the kind florist?
Who slides down the staircase now
And can I still climb to the roof to raise the flag?
Whose feet scurry through the halls
As crystal chinks and father tries to outwit peeping Toms
Has the court been overtaken by moss
No balls wing their way back and forth
No agile feet run or stroll the gardens, I muse.
Your manicured terraces afforded playing grounds
But the gorge frightened me
Even as the bridge allowed passage.
Is the tree still lit at Christmas?
And the jackfruit, yes, the jackfruit!
Evidence stuck on our lips and hands
Provoking scoldings first then lashings
A mien of cleanliness and innocence obtained
From gas siphoned from parked Pontiacs and Bentleys.
Yes, we cleaned up well and good.
We surely did----

Flexing cricking shoulders
Replacing misty spectacles
Righting a stoop with a staff,
She stands alone by the mountainside
To ask questions of no one
And recalls memories others would soon forget.

Ottawa, 1978

The River

Ariveris
amassofwater
collectingdebris
eatingawaytheland
overflowingitsbanks
andeventhatthatisbeautiful.

A river is a
a mass of water
collecting debris
eating away the land
overflowing its banks
and even that is beautiful.

A river is my love
With its ripplings, sighings and lappings
Its soothings and engulfing
Its conquerings of new frontiers.
A river is the lion's roaring fierceness
Or catlike stealth
Overpowering

          Devouring
Provoking frenzied quiverings
Not submission this --
Not supplication either
And if you suggest domination --
On whose part --?

My love beckons --
 I comply.
That, is my river!

                              Carleton U, 1978

Fare-well

Here, deep, deep down on the earth lie snow battlefields.
There, deep, deep in the ground repose the buried bones of
my father;
 -- Ashes to ash and dust to dust --
Who will tell me I speak a lie?
Will you tell me I speak false?
Or will I tell myself?
Again and again I have heard repeated
Your father died on a Friday
Five days after Christmas.
He couldn't wait to embrace the New Year!
He said his last good-bye to the old
Performing his last task and act
Returning to his native home.

     His bones now rest in peace
     His spirit flies over to me
     And curbs my restlessness.

I did not throw in some soil
Being thousands of miles away.

     It is all a part of me
Pictures cloud each other
     Engage me for a moment
     Then, are gone!
     I sit back and try to capture them --
     What are they -- those flitting images --
     They evade my memory and leave me cold
     Cold from the deprivation of sight
     Cold from the fear of loneliness
     And the barrenness that surrounds me
     Frozen like the rain pelting down on me
     Making my life miserable and meaningless.

I couldn't see you to say goodbye
My last farewell left unsaid --
Hangs in the air;
Between us so much left unsaid
But you have always known my mind
And I have always known yours
So, a part of me lies buried with you
Even as I try to survive this endless snow
These biting bitter winds of Carleton!

I stand at the foot of my father's grave
Shake my head in disbelief
Whether for what could have been or should
I do not know.
Straws are too fragile for thought
This is as it should be.
Is dying not inherent in living?
Why persist in questioning?
What answer is ever enough or right?

Carleton U, Ottawa, January 24, 1979

Le Bosquet

Thank you Sons and Daughters of Africa
                              p i p i n g o u t y o u r s o u l s
Straining at haphazard tables
Grinning at each other
Tapping to the beat --
As Misse gripped
-- Il a pris toute la soiree --
The drums and guitars and horns complained and pulsed
The thrilling cadence in song
Beat of Africa
Heat and heart of Africa
Continent of amoebic temperament
Sizzling with Life
Bursting at the seams
Overflowing with nourishment
And calling back your children
While Nchakounte invented Maghambo
                              and Retro
Come play my xylophone, drums and flute –
Come shake my shakers
Come blow my elephant horn
Come tie my ancestral cowries and beads
Let us pay tribute where it is due!
Speak to me talking drum of Africa
Whisper your secrets softly in my ear!
Whisper, whisper, whisper again and again
Oh Mother Africa so I may never forget
Whisper so I will forever remember,
Whisper so they will never forget,
Gyrating backsides and wriggling waistlines
Testimonials of jubilant participation

Spectacle of long forgotten village squares
Now acquiescing to measured frenzied step.
I am happy for this moment!

Douala 1980 (on vacation)

Midnight Girl

She hangs around the corner,
Waiting for the drifters --
At last, she finds herself in business--
The poor victim finds himself
                    in a dingy upstairs bedroom,
peeling off her clothes --
To discover the concealed crevices
                    in her sagging and layered body.

Douala, 1980

Menchum

The fall falls from out the sky
Thundering down the gorge
Foaming, vanishing, rising skyward
As it makes sweet music
We watch, mesmerized
See our bodies' sink, then rise in unison
Merge, effervesce, and disintegrate.
Quiet surrounds, trees lean to perceive
Rocks cry out in agreement at such battering
Birds marvel, executing competing dives

One lone pebble disappears into this softness
Its cry for help absorbed in the thundering!
Watch the children watch and wonder and marvel
As the fall falls from out the sky
See them catch the rainbow ---
Then cautiously step back to avoid the precipice
History and geography lessons recalled
Could this be the fall?
Believed powerful enough to light up Africa?
Now become our playground ---
Chump! Ch-u-m-ph! Ch-u-m-ph!
I can make the biggest splash!
No. That was not a splash!
See me make the splash!
Do you call that a splash!
I, I am the champion!
Sounds of children frolicking in quiet running streams ---
Arise and be baptized at the fall
As the fall falls from out the sky
And sinks into the earth!
      Or/h/h! Sinking, falling, never to rise
      in the depths of dark forgotten Africa.

Buffalo, 1981

Mother Nyos

Was it for Death you called us back!
Compromised,
         We saw love and care --
Deceived by lush enticing greenery
Ripe juicy mangoes, solo papaya, buttery avocadoes and
mouth watering pineapples
Juices coursing down firm quivering chins,
Juices in-roading restless fingers and youthful hearts
Savory timbanaboosas, tasty foofoo, huckleberry and katikati,
Bibles of the land, luring --
Entranced contemplations of rolling hills
Could Splendor be more permanent, we asked.
Certainly, never more reassuring!
The
   calm
      of
       your
`   blue
              waters
Rumbling, Gassing, Choking, Burning, Killing --
Was it for this you beckoned your children back to you?
Tricking and summoning to a mortal embrace!!

                        Yaounde, 1986

The Kola-Nut

 North, South, East, West
Kola knows no boundaries --
Kola has no color, yes I say
It has no color
No Religions
No Ethnic groups --
It is friendship
It is Welcome
It is Unity
It is Peace.
Kola is LIFE.
If you break kola with me
Then you cannot break me.
If you break kola with me
It follows I am your friend.
But you, you break kola with me
Then nab my woman;
You, you break kola with me
And turn and grab my man;
You are what you eat!
Keep what you have nabbed and grabbed
Taste the ash of suspended confrontation
Swim in the mired thrill of remembered battles, Friend!
For this, this is my kola to you.

Yaounde, 1990

Ode to Farmers

You toil and toil and toil
You work and work and work
You sweat all day in the heat of the Sun
You plant your cocoa then nurse it,
You plant your coffee, tend it
Your cotton
      palms
      bananas
      rubber
      You cherish all --
These nurturings bear fruit.
Was all this work, work, and work for nothing
Is that what your life's sweat is!
NOTHING
You shiver all night from the pains of your labor
And not an aspirin can you get
'Cos your labor has gone unpaid
No! No! No!
You must be paid for all your Toil
You must be remunerated for your sweat
For your coffee
      your cocoa
      your cotton
      palms
      rubber
      bananas
You must be paid
And not later -- You will be paid
 -- NOW --

Back home to withered hungry faces

Every evening you return
Honor, Respect -- ALL, GONE
Outstanding fees still unpaid
Not a decent dress for the wife
Nor shoes to shod your callused feet
'Cos your labors have remained unpaid
Meanwhile echoes of Marble Castles, we hear
Where gold and silver adorn
Where oozing sweat stinks of Champagne
Here, The Reapers are not the Sowers of your humble Toil
With holidays in the Bahamas
With Silk for 'kerchiefs
Crocodiles do shoe the feet
While hungry you go to bed
Unfed -- to die your Death
'Cos your labors have gone unpaid
How many corpses of you
To give you your due!!!!!

Yaounde March 29, 1991

Africa in Miniature

Amputations and disputations
Accusations and then counters
And woe betide those of differing leanings --
This is what Politics is made of
                 Cameroon style of course!!
Hisan Habre's volunteers massacre with impunity
Sisters, mothers, brothers, fathers, all exploited
Their land expropriated
Volunteers trained in the nether lands of Djoum
By experts from the promise land.
Boastfully proclaiming Africa in miniature
Ain't that the truth --I say
From South Africa to Zaire, to Benin, to the horn
Even as far as the Mediterranean
Nothing but disputation—
Nothing but genocide—
Why should Cameroon be different?
It is only Africa in miniature
A geriatric ward crowded with infusion tubes and bags,
Half-baked knighted politicians and partisan journalists
Woe betide you for differing political leanings
Woe betide you for voicing a singular opinion
You have sold out to the enemy
You have deceived your public
Accusations labelled by former henchmen of now enemy
party
Come elections, bags of rice weigh both down
Drums of oil grease not only SUVs but palms
Former brittle shin bones and lips now luminous
Rumors of ballot stuffing and multiple voting abound
Who is deceiving who?

Say what you will,
There will be no debate!!!!!!

Yaounde, 1992

Whitesands of Mombassa

Distant beaches, distant shores
Distant ships on the fathomless horizon
Distant visitors on Whitesands--
Ah! Whitesands in the heat of the Sun
White foam of the Indes
Come caress my thighs
Clothe me with your splendors.

In your wake, shells galore
                  Miniscule,
                    Beautiful --
Vendors of Kangas and Kitenges at triple the price
Displayed on Whitesands
Distant boats call out too, whistling--
Shall we go snorkeling?
Shall you go water-skiing?
I can take you scuba diving --

Waving off offers on we ambulate
Strangers yet not so on these distant shores
Flinging in half-baked "jambos" and "Hakuna Matatas"
We are not Muzungo -- We are Africans
We cannot be cheated, not by you
By you with the retreating back
And the now flat feet at midday
You will return unasked
Beating down the beaches
Prohibiting my midnight walks
Restricting ramblings to high walls of Whitesands
Spitting out rotted coconut shells
On these not so so distant beaches

On these present shores,
On these white sands.

Mombassa, June 1994

The Rainmaker

Cut down your bushes
Cut them down
Right to the ground!
And the thistles and thorns rebelled
Fortified by weeping skies
And grew to great height and mass
Jealous of the Sun.
How the women groaned at this abundance--
Old men sighed, gnashing teeth
Contemplating blisters and aching muscles
Tottering over callused gnarled feet and hands
Glaring at boisterous finely moulded youth
Who pranced and preened in firm show-off
Gleaming keen machetes caught the Sun
And sticks wiggled in a show of force in the earth

I say staffs were dancing in abandon
As the young maidens applauded and giggled
While mothers identified Sons and Sons-to-be
And old men moaned at such naked power
Yes, Old men groaned in dismay and discomfort at such
exuberance
Coveting fresh unending defiance --
 Oh! Contemplating youth scampered in glee
Dreaming of evolutions and revolutions

But, insisting boisterous youthful voices rang out in chant
Cut down your bushes
Cut them down—
                Right
to
   the
     ground
Then, pile up the grasses
Pile them up, right to the Sky
Then, Burn them DOWN!
Burn them down right to the ground
And scatter your seeds to the cry of the Rainmaker.

                        Ottawa 1976,
                        Buea, 1995

A New Day

"Cash," I say, welcome back."
Welcome to post Election Day.
What happened to the "see" machine?
Were the brakes faulty?
Crazy machine zapping downhill
On democracy's speed-brake-less advanced highway
Ploughing mousy web-like villages
Raising bustling loquacious cities
Undermining transitions and adjustments.
Tomorrow, I will tell you to shut up
I will exhort you to bask in your borrowed robes
Praying you not discover what the Emperor did,
I want no suicide on my conscience
I am an old man simply waiting out my days-
I am a mini-skirted, midi-length wearing young girl
I will rain down curses on you
I am not as soft-spoken as my mother.
Beware and Be weary.

6-11-97

34

Call me ---

I will till my soil and plant my seeds --
I will pay you no mind
Call me what you will --
I will weed God's grass and nurse my corn.
--Have you nothing better to do? --
Come June, I will harvest my maize
I will roast my corn by the roadside
I will sell and you will buy.
Call me no more Names.
If you will sell your land
I, I will buy my land
I will crown my apartments
You will seek shelter under my roof
I will not deny you this
Just as I did not deny you corn.
Your children and forebears count diminishing pennies
Surrendering to a settler population.

As I tilled the soil
You called me names
Then sashayed past as I planted my seeds
--Dirty job for country folk --
Did I issue a rebuke!
I shared my produce in times of hunger.
Granted, I sold, you bought!
But what did you do while I labored?
In ceaseless rains I worked,
Under scorching skies I sweated.
Come June, I will select the fattest corn
 These, I will eat with my children
The rest, I will sell to you --

And having no other choice you will buy --

So, call me names no more!
But, if you must,
Wouldn't it be nice to say "Master?
                              Brother
                              Sister?

Buea, 6-11-97

Call me: A variation

I will till my soil
                          And plant my seeds
I will pay you no mind
Call me what you will

I will weed God's grass and nurse my corn
--Have you nothing better to do --

Come June, I will harvest my maize
                  I will roast my corn by the roadside
                  I will sell and you will buy

Call me no more names.
If you will sell your land
I
I will buy my land

I will crown my apartments
You will seek shelter under my roof

Your children
                  And forebears
                              count diminishing pennies
Surrendering to a settler population--

As I tilled the soil
You called me names
Then sashayed past as I planted my seeds
--dirty job for country folk--

Did I issue a rebuke!

I shared my produce in times of hunger
I shared my produce in times of hunger
Granted, I sold and you bought
But what were you doing while I labored

Under scorching skies
                    I sweated
In ceaseless rains
                    I ploughed

Come June, I will select the fattest corn

These I will eat with my children

The rest, I will sell to you
--And having no other choice
                         you will buy--

So, call me names no more

But, if you must,
Wouldn't it be nice to say
                    MASTER, NO.
                    BROTHER, WELL!
                    SISTER? YES.

6-11-97

Election fragments

Speak to me Yamasoukourou
Basilica devoted to worship
Architecture resounding with fear and greed
Love, money and robbery stand
Piled one onto the other
While Bouake basks in nature's threads
In castoff zinc houses lining sandy and dusty roads
Is this Africa –

Dubreka is quiet and dark on election night
I can hear neither her voice nor her music
Only aluminium drills and hiccoughs
As we scurry for candles and aladdin lamps
For why has power outage happened only now--
Boxes emptied and cast ballots on the table
Ballots which determine whether change will occur
Change that determines Africa's future!

But the bare-footed lady in Antsirabe
Traipsed some twelve miles, ballot box in hand
Having vowed to make her voice heard
She was all for change, yes change!
Madam President of the polling station
She believed change was non-negotiable
And it was about time too!!
That set us all roaring, each clamoring for audience
So yes her shoed husband by her side ensured her safety
Recalled happenings of nearby eras
When men ruled and had prominence
Or thought they did, but we knew better.

A Perfect Setting

In the lodge a log fire dominates
Commands the center as shivering lambs huddle --
A cackling fire fends off the cold
While for a quick warm-up local bottles of fire abound
Chairs scattered every which way
Mementos of offspring displayed prominently
Old Roger snores by the fireside
And Kitty chases after unforeseen mice
And I think this is a perfect setting for a meeting.

In the kitchen a woman screams in hurt
She has burned herself with the pot
Been cooking all day long
Been rushed off her feet all day long
She has pounded and boiled and fried
She can barely stand
But she insists-
It is her job to supply the food
It is her job to nurture and promote growth.

Behold the man on the verandah
The head of the household,
The breadwinner
His legs crossed at the ankles
He leans back in his cane chair
Puffing on his pipe and reading yesterday's paper
For he is yesterday's man.

But, in the lodge
The chairs stand at attention
With eight perfect place settings
Clean and bright and beckoning,
A well-trimmed fire simmers and glows and cackles
As more logs are fed in to ensure continuity,
And saucepans boil over and sizzle-
And aromas waft through the air-
And we salivate and run to wash hands-
And my overworked and under-appreciated Ma
Beams to welcome her children home
Proclaiming not tiredness but care
And I say, this, this is indeed a perfect setting for a family
dinner.

Buea, 2000

A Lament II

Silence -------
Thundering silence ----
A scampering for cover
A dash for the darkest corner
A merging with the floor?
To kiss not the earth
Rather to cement an embrace
Plunging with the volley
Gymnastics relegated to pre-teen years
My nose out of joint
Helter, skelter, destination unknown
I had forgotten the cupboard
Now, I sport a one-lens frame
My locks suggest the strange order of Rastafa
Shoeless, we take to our heels,
Shirts, pants, skirts, blouses and loincloths awry,
The neighborhood is on the street,
Marveling at the monstrous majestic inferno
Provoking a dilemma of questioning!
Whither your path, my friend!
Should we take flight or brave it out and see,
For we are doubting Thomases
And books do not always carry the complete message of
God.

My once eternal home rocks us to the ground,
Bids us recollect forgotten sacrifices of albinos,
Strange offerings to a stranger god,
Who to bequeath life must expropriate life!
Where, *Epasa Moto*, is meaning?
Must we cry out like the forgotten bones of your children,

Twins of yesteryears abandoned in your forests
Forsaken by parents to rot as none heed our howl,
None but the wolves who make mince meat of our fragile
bones!
Must all "come-no-goes" bag and baggage in hand
Retreat to the highlands from which they came!
For we are afraid and my little girl speaks for us
When she says, "Let us take the dog and goat and leave this
place."
And yet, we have become a part of this earth,
We remain a part of you!
Will you welcome us or reject us?

Buea, 2000

Lawino's daughter's song

Calling to my sisters and cousins I am already on my way
Having prepared and left the morning and noon meals at home
For my Lord and master, and the babies!
Having heated water and called him to bathe
Having given the young a rub down;
For I beat the cock to it every morn
THIS is woman's work!
My body aches, but I cannot complain.
My back needs a massage
But with no one to give it I grin and bear it.
My man has no time for such trivialities!

I pile the grass and burn
Throw in a potato or coco yam and smother it with ash,
This will be my noon meal
I dig all the daylong and make ridges and furrows,
Then, put in some bean and corn seeds.
Months from now if the heavens are generous
I will return to pull out the weeds;
For this is my office and I must keep it clean
Embracing the economics of demand and supply.
This too is woman's work!

Climbing hills, descending valleys, "kenjas" on my back
I return not to rest;
Gourds balanced on my head and calabashes in my hands
I return not to rest;
To the stream I must proceed to fetch water to bathe
I must fetch water to cook the evening meal
I must fetch water to bathe the children

I must fetch enough water so my man can bathe!
For this, this is woman's work!

I hear my daughters speak of Beijing, Mother
And wonder what it all means
For they live in the city and tell me
That even here a woman has her work cut out for her!
A man and a woman may both leave the house each morning
But returning at 5 o'clock it is the woman
The woman who dons a kabba
Goes to the kitchen to light the stove
Bring the pot to a boil
Put the food on the table,
Throw the clothes in the machine (if there is one)
Don't ask me what happens if there isn't one
For you and I both know the answer to that!
Brooms too must have their own say in the house
Cobwebs must come down;
For isn't this too her office!
But how many offices can one woman have?
How many economies manage?
No wonder, a woman's work is never done!
To her satisfaction, that is,
For she is a perfectionist and expects only the best
For she is a woman with know-how,
Patient
Enduring
Resilient
And beautiful!
And do not ask her how come?
She just IS.

She curtsies and she dips

She falls from out the sky, does she!
No! She glides and waves and dances
She dips and curtsies
She sighs and s I g h s
Then blows and rains down kisses
And flies and flies and flies.
Yes, she falls and glides and waves
Then beckons and dances a waltz
To dream and dream of waves and --
Nothing

Buea, 2003

The Letter

I am hungry for you tonight
I want you tonight
I need you tonight.
Hungerwantneed intertwine like torsos
Fight and play leg like then arm like
I want your arms around me tonight
I need to be squeezed tight tonight
To know that you can chase my ghosts away
For I am lonely tonight
And needs like no other
Breathe back my lifeline
Hunger will feed want
Want will answer need
Need satisfy hunger

And U are hungry for me tonight
U need me tonight
U want me tonight
Hunger want and need spark a fire
Hunger, need accede the ground
Nothing but want, want, want
Only hunger want want need and then some more
And you are alive
And my ghosts are no more

I have absorbed life from you
Hunger will feed hunger
Want answer want
Need demonstrate need
And we are hungry for each other
Giving each other life.

Read and give me back my life!

The Lady said "No" today!
What Lady?
That Lady? Like all ladies
She has denied me her splendours
She has flirted with me all day long
But remained true to her own god
Clouded in multiple layers and shapes of veils
Oh! That she would dance just for a peep –
Today, I looked up and she was bald
Stripped of her greenery
Burned down beyond recognition
Said to usher in the rains
I wondered why the coyness and sighed.

Buea, 2003

Dance of the Vampire

When you danced the dance of the vampires
When chameleon-like you robe and disrobe
When you have sold kith and kin
To weigh down your pockets
Look not around!
All invitees search for other tasks
They cannot come to the party
Who wants to carouse with the vampire?

There was a time …
Yes! There was a time for chi-chatting
A time for backstabbing
And chickens must come home to roost
Your seeds were defective …
No! They were poisoned seeds
Arsenic will only welcome death
And you are not simply dead
You are Death!!
S-o-f-t-l-y you stole entrance
Your sugared tongue admission fee
As you swayed to the rhythm
Dancing the dance of the vampires
What music touched your soul?
Was there ever a rhythm to your dance?
The dance of no sound
The music of no instrument
Bow to your silence of destruction
And drink of your own blood
The story Bram dared not write!

Buea, 2003

49

Waves

No gentle lapping waves I see before me
No quiet in which to think my thoughts
Play catch with man's faithful companion, Roger
Or young architects to construct elaborate sand castles
Where young lovers strut and cajole each other to convince
In the wrinkles of young laughter
The beach has disappeared
Angry foam and froth beat the embankment
As if to ask why its journey must stop here
For some this is not enough
They rise above the embankment
Splash and spit their anger on man, woman and child
Then sighing, reel in sand, stone, grass, shells, all
And slither back down the embankment.

What shaped your majestic beauty!
What your undulations!
Crowned your abode with riches of fishes
Fish that sparkle and fade in simple frolic
Fins that expand, contract in joyful refrain
Stars, like the fish, darting in and out
Piercing the waters in pleasant frolic
Shredding my heart to pieces
And sucking my life blood away!
Yes, every Christmas day we pretended to swim
The undertow almost sucking my brother away
Children making claims they could not live up to.

Buea, 2003